from *Life on the Mississippi*
Mark Twain

LOOKING FORWARD

When young Mark Twain's hopes of striking it rich in South America are dashed, he sets out to follow his boyhood dream: becoming a steamboat pilot.

© 2002 Perfection Learning® Corporation
1000 North Second Avenue, P.O. Box 500, Logan, Iowa 51546-0500
Tel: 1-800-831-4190 • Fax: 1-800-543-2745
ISBN 0-7891-5746-2
perfectionlearning.com
Printed in the U.S.A.

3 4 5 6 7 8 PP 11 10 09 08 07 06

WORDS TO WATCH FOR

Here are some words that may be unfamiliar. Use this list as a guide to better understanding. Examine it before you begin to read.

abstruse—hard to understand; complex
homage—respect; reverence
ignoble—low; mean; dishonorable
imminent—approaching; soon to happen
obscurity—darkness; oblivion
plaintive—sad; mournful
prodigious—immense; tremendous
prudence—wisdom; good judgment
transient—temporary; fleeting
sublime—lofty; inspiring

from *Life on the Mississippi*
by Mark Twain

The Boys' Ambition

When I was a boy, there was but one permanent ambition among my comrades in our village[1] on the west bank of the Mississippi River. That was, to be a steamboatman. We had transient ambitions of other sorts, but they were only transient. When a circus came and went, it left us all burning to become clowns; the first negro minstrel show that ever came to our section left us all suffering to try that kind of life; now and then we had a hope that, if we lived and were good, God would permit us to be pirates. These ambitions faded out, each in its turn; but the ambition to be a steamboatman always remained.

Once a day a cheap, gaudy packet arrived upward from St. Louis, and another downward from Keokuk. Before these events, the day was glorious with expectancy; after them, the day was a dead and empty thing. Not only the boys, but the whole village, felt this. After all these years I can picture that old time to myself now, just as it was then: the white town drowsing in the sunshine of a summer's morning; the streets empty, or pretty nearly so; one or

---

[1] *village*: Hannibal, Missouri

two clerks sitting in front of the Water Street stores, with their splint-bottomed chairs tilted back against the walls, chins on breasts, hats slouched over their faces, asleep—with shingle-shavings enough around to show what broke them down; a sow and a litter of pigs loafing along the sidewalk, doing a good business in watermelon rinds and seeds; two or three lonely little freight piles scattered about the "levee";[2] a pile of "skids"[3] on the slope of the stone-paved wharf, and the fragrant town drunkard asleep in the shadow of them; two or three wood flats at the head of the wharf, but nobody to listen to the peaceful lapping of the wavelets against them; the great Mississippi, the majestic, the magnificent Mississippi, rolling its mile-wide tide along, shining in the sun; the dense forest away on the other side; the "point" above the town, and the "point" below, bounding the river-glimpse and turning it into a sort of sea, and withal a very still and brilliant and lonely one. Presently a film of dark smoke appears above one of those remote "points": instantly a negro drayman,[4] famous for his quick eye and prodigious voice, lifts up the cry, "S-t-e-a-m-boat a-comin'!" and the scene changes! The town drunkard

---

[2] *levee*: a ridge of land that prevents flooding

[3] *skids*: wooden fenders

[4] *drayman*: one who hauls goods using a wooden cart without sides

stirs, the clerks wake up, a furious clatter of drays follows, every house and store pours out a human contribution, and all in a twinkling the dead town is alive and moving. Drays, carts, men, boys, all go hurrying from many quarters to a common center, the wharf. Assembled there, the people fasten their eyes upon the coming boat as upon a wonder they are seeing for the first time. And the boat *is* rather a handsome sight, too. She is long and sharp and trim and pretty; she has two tall, fancy-topped chimneys, with a gilded device of some kind swung between them; a fanciful pilot-house, all glass and "gingerbread," perched on top of the "texas" deck behind them; the paddle-boxes are gorgeous with a picture or with gilded rays above the boat's name; the boiler-deck, the hurricane-deck, and the texas deck are fenced and ornamented with clean white railings; there is a flag gallantly flying from the jack-staff; the furnace doors are open and the fires glaring bravely; the upper decks are black with passengers; the captain stands by the big bell, calm, imposing, the envy of all; great volumes of the blackest smoke are rolling and tumbling out of the chimneys—a husbanded grandeur created with a bit of pitch-pine just before arriving at a town; the crew are grouped on the forecastle; the broad stage is run far out over the port bow, and an envied deck-hand stands picturesquely on the end of it with a coil of rope in his hand; the pent steam is screaming through the gauge-cocks; the captain lifts his hand, a bell rings, the wheels stop; then they turn back, churning the water to foam, and the steamer is at rest. Then such a scramble as there is to get aboard, and to get ashore, and to take in freight and to discharge freight, all at one and the same time; and such a yelling and cursing as the mates facilitate it all with! Ten minutes later the steamer is under way again, with no flag on the jack-staff and no black smoke issuing from the chimneys. After ten more minutes the town is dead again, and the town drunkard asleep by the skids once more.

My father was a justice of the peace, and I supposed he possessed the power of life and death over all men, and could hang anybody that offended him. This was distinction enough for me as a general thing; but the desire to be a steamboatman kept intruding, nevertheless. I first wanted to be a cabin-boy, so that I could come out with a white apron and shake a table-cloth over the side, where all my old comrades could see me; later I thought I would rather be the deck-hand who stood on the end of the stage-plank with the coil of rope in his hand, because he was particularly conspicuous. But these were only day-dreams—they were too heavenly to be contemplated as real possibilities. By and by one of our boys went away. He was not heard of for a long time. At last he turned up as apprentice engineer or "striker" on a steamboat. This thing shook the bottom out of all my Sunday-school teachings. That boy had been notoriously worldly, and I just the reverse; yet he was exalted to this eminence, and I left in obscurity and misery. There was nothing generous about this fellow in his greatness. He would always manage to have a rusty bolt to scrub while his boat tarried at our town, and he would sit on the inside guard and scrub it, where we all could see him and envy him and loathe him. And whenever his boat was laid up he would come home and swell around the town in his blackest and greasiest clothes, so that nobody could help remembering that he was a steamboatman; and he used all sorts of steamboat technicalities in his talk, as if he were so used to them that he forgot common people could not understand them. He would speak of the "labboard" side of a horse in an easy, natural way that would make one wish he was dead. And he was always talking about "St. Looy" like an old citizen; he would refer casually to occasions when he was "coming down Fourth Street," or when he was "passing by the Planter's House," or when there was a fire and he took a turn on the brakes of "the old

Big Missouri"; and then he would go on and lie about how many towns the size of ours were burned down there that day. Two or three of the boys had long been persons of consideration among us because they had been to St. Louis once and had a vague general knowledge of its wonders, but the day of their glory was over now. They lapsed into a humble silence, and learned to disappear when the ruthless "cub"-engineer approached. This fellow had money, too, and hair-oil. Also an ignorant silver watch and a showy brass watch-chain. He wore a leather belt and used no suspenders. If ever a youth was cordially admired and hated by his comrades, this one was. No girl could withstand his charms. He "cut out" every boy in the village. When his boat blew up at last, it diffused a tranquil contentment among us such as we had not known for months. But when he came home the next week, alive, renowned, and appeared in church all battered up and bandaged, a shining hero, stared at and wondered over by everybody, it seemed to us that the partiality of Providence for an undeserving reptile had reached a point where it was open to criticism.

This creature's career could produce but one result, and it speedily followed. Boy after boy managed to get on the river. The minister's son became an engineer. The doctor's and the postmaster's sons became "mud clerks";[5] the wholesale liquor dealer's son became a barkeeper on a boat; four sons of the chief merchant, and two sons of the county judge, became pilots. Pilot was the grandest position of all. The pilot, even in those days of trivial wages, had a princely salary—from a hundred and fifty to two hundred and fifty dollars a month, and no board to pay. Two months of his wages would pay a preacher's salary for a year. Now some of us were left disconsolate. We could not get on the river—at least our parents would not let us.

So, by and by, I ran away. I said I would never come home again till I was a pilot and could come in glory. But somehow I could not manage it. I went meekly aboard a few of the boats that lay packed together like sardines at the long St. Louis wharf, and humbly inquired for the pilots, but got only a cold shoulder and short words from mates and clerks. I had to make the best of this sort of treatment for the time being, but I had comforting daydreams of a future when I should be a great and honored pilot, with plenty of money, and could kill some of these mates and clerks and pay for them.

I Want to Be a Cub-Pilot

---

[5] *mud clerks*: unsalaried crew members who are responsible for the comfort and welfare of passengers

Months afterward the hope within me struggled to a reluctant death, and I found myself without an ambition. But I was ashamed to go home. I was in Cincinnati, and I set to work to map out a new career. I had been reading about the recent exploration of the river Amazon by an expedition sent out by our government. It was said that the expedition, owing to difficulties, had not thoroughly explored a part of the country lying about the headwaters, some four thousand miles from the mouth of the river. It was only about fifteen hundred miles from Cincinnati to New Orleans, where I could doubtless get a ship. I had thirty dollars left; I would go and complete the exploration of the Amazon. This was all the thought I gave to the subject. I never was great in matters of detail. I packed my valise,[6] and took passage on an ancient tub called the *Paul Jones*, for New Orleans. For the sum of sixteen dollars I had the scarred and tarnished splendors of "her" main saloon principally to myself, for she was not a creature to attract the eye of wiser travelers.

When we presently got under way and went poking down the broad Ohio, I became a new being, and the subject of my own admiration. I was a traveler! A word never had tasted so good in my mouth before. I had an exultant sense of being bound for

---

[6] *valise*: suitcase

mysterious lands and distant climes[7] which I never have felt in so uplifting a degree since. I was in such a glorified condition that all ignoble feelings departed out of me, and I was able to look down and pity the untraveled with a compassion that had hardly a trace of contempt in it. Still, when we stopped at villages and wood-yards, I could not help lolling carelessly upon the railings of the boiler-deck to enjoy the envy of the country boys on the bank. If they did not seem to discover me, I presently sneezed to attract their attention, or moved to a position where they could not help seeing me. And as soon as I knew they saw me I gaped and stretched, and gave other signs of being mightily bored with traveling.

I kept my hat off all the time, and stayed where the wind and the sun could strike me, because I wanted to get the bronzed and weather-beaten look of an old traveler. Before the second day was half gone I experienced a joy which filled me with the purest gratitude; for I saw that the skin had begun to blister and peel off my face and neck. I wished that the boys and girls at home could see me now.

We reached Louisville in time—at least the neighborhood of it. We stuck hard and fast on the rocks in the middle of the river, and lay there four days. I was now beginning to feel a strong sense of being a

---

[7] *climes*: climates

part of the boat's family, a sort of infant son to the captain and younger brother to the officers. There is no estimating the pride I took in this grandeur, or the affection that began to swell and grow in me for those people. I could not know how the lordly steamboatman scorns that sort of presumption in a mere landsman. I particularly longed to acquire the least trifle of notice from the big stormy mate, and I was on the alert for an opportunity to do him a service to that end. It came at last. The riotous powwow of setting a spar was going on down on the forecastle, and I went down there and stood around in the way—or mostly skipping out of it—till the mate suddenly roared a general order for somebody to bring him a capstan bar.[8] I sprang to his side and said: "Tell me where it is—I'll fetch it!"

If a rag-picker[9] had offered to do a diplomatic service for the Emperor of Russia, the monarch could not have been more astounded than the mate was. He even stopped swearing. He stood and stared down at me. It took him ten seconds to scrape his disjointed remains together again. Then he said impressively: "Well, if this don't beat h—l!" and turned to his work with the air of a man who had

---

[8] *capstan bar*: a lever used to operate a capstan, which is a rotating machine used to raise or lower heavy objects, especially from a ship

[9] *rag-picker*: one who collects used rags and other unwanted items for a living

been confronted with a problem too abstruse for solution.

I crept away, and courted solitude for the rest of the day. I did not go to dinner; I stayed away from supper until everybody else had finished. I did not feel so much like a member of the boat's family now as before. However, my spirits returned, in installments, as we pursued our way down the river. I was sorry I hated the mate so, because it was not in (young) human nature not to admire him. He was huge and muscular, his face was bearded and whiskered all over; he had a red woman and a blue woman tattooed on his right arm—one on each side of a blue anchor with a red rope to it; and in the matter of profanity he was sublime. When he was getting out cargo at a landing, I was always where I could see and hear. He felt all the majesty of his great position, and made the world feel it, too. When he gave even the simplest order, he discharged it like a blast of lightning, and sent a long, reverberating peal of profanity thundering after it. I could not help contrasting the way in which the average landsman would give an order with the mate's way of doing it. If the landsman should wish the gangplank moved a foot farther forward, he would probably say: "James, or William, one of you push that plank forward, please"; but put the mate in his place, and he would roar out: "Here, now, start that gang-plank for'ard! Lively, now! *What*'re you about! Snatch it! *snatch* it! There! there! Aft again! aft again! Don't you hear me? Dash it to dash! are you going to *sleep* over it! '*Vast* heaving. 'Vast heaving, I tell you! Going to heave it clear astern? WHERE're you going with that barrel! *for'ard* with it 'fore I make you swallow it, you dash-dash-dash-*dashed* split between a tired mud-turtle and a crippled hearse-horse!"

I wished I could talk like that.

When the soreness of my adventure with the mate had somewhat worn off, I began timidly to make up to the humblest official connected with the boat— the night watchman. He snubbed my advances at first, but I presently ventured to offer him a new chalk pipe, and that softened him. So he allowed me to sit with him by the big bell on the hurricane-deck, and in time he melted into conversation. He could not well have helped it, I hung with such homage on his words and so plainly showed that I felt honored by his notice. He told me the names of dim capes and shadowy islands as we glided by them in the solemnity of the night, under the winking stars, and by and by got to talking about himself. He seemed over-sentimental for a man whose salary was six dollars a week—or rather he might have seemed so to an older person than I. But I drank in his words hungrily, and with a faith that might have moved mountains if it had been applied judiciously. What was it to me that he was soiled and seedy and fragrant with gin? What was it to me that his grammar was bad, his construction worse, and his profanity so void of art that it was an element of weakness rather than strength in his conversation? He was a wronged man, a man who had seen trouble, and that was enough for me. As he mellowed into his plaintive history his tears dripped upon the lantern in his lap, and I cried, too, from sympathy. He said he was the son of an English nobleman—either an earl or an alderman, he could not remember which, but believed was both; his father, the nobleman, loved him, but his mother hated him from the cradle; and so while he was still a little boy he was sent to "one of them old, ancient colleges"—he couldn't remember which; and by and by his father died and his mother seized the property and "shook" him, as he phrased it. After his mother shook him, members of the nobility with whom he was acquainted used their influence to get him the position of "loblolly-boy[10] in a ship"; and from that point my watchman threw off all trammels of date and locality and branched out into a narrative that bristled all along with incredible adventures; a narrative that was so

---

[10] *loblolly-boy*: chef in charge of making gruel

reeking with bloodshed, and so crammed with hairbreadth escapes and the most engaging and unconscious personal villainies, that I sat speechless, enjoying, shuddering, wondering, worshiping.

It was a sore blight to find out afterward that he was a low, vulgar, ignorant, sentimental, half-witted humbug, an untraveled native of the wilds of Illinois, who had absorbed wildcat literature and appropriated its marvels, until in time he had woven odds and ends of the mess into this yarn, and then gone on telling it to fledglings like me, until he had come to believe it himself.

A Cub-Pilot's Experience

What with lying on the rocks four days at Louisville, and some other delays, the poor old *Paul Jones* fooled away about two weeks in making the voyage from Cincinnati to New Orleans. This gave me a chance to get acquainted with one of the pilots, and he taught me how to steer the boat, and thus made the fascination of river life more potent than ever for me.

It also gave me a chance to get acquainted with a youth who had taken deck passage[11]—more's the pity; for he easily borrowed six dollars of me on a promise to return to the boat and pay it back to me

---

[11] *deck passage*: accomodations for the lowest-paying passengers

the day after we should arrive. But he probably died or forgot, for he never came. It was doubtless the former, since he had said his parents were wealthy, and he only traveled deck passage because it was cooler.

I soon discovered two things. One was that a vessel would not be likely to sail for the mouth of the Amazon under ten or twelve years; and the other was that the nine or ten dollars still left in my pocket would not suffice for so impossible an exploration as I had planned, even if I could afford to wait for a ship. Therefore it followed that I must contrive a new career. The *Paul Jones* was now bound for St. Louis. I planned a siege against my pilot, and at the end of three hard days he surrendered. He agreed to teach me the Mississippi River from New Orleans to St. Louis for five hundred dollars, payable out of the first wages I should receive after graduating. I entered upon the small enterprise of "learning" twelve or thirteen hundred miles of the great Mississippi River with the easy confidence of my time of life. If I had really known what I was about to require of my faculties, I should not have had the courage to begin. I supposed that all a pilot had to do was to keep his boat in the river, and I did not consider that that could be much of a trick, since it was so wide.

The boat backed out from New Orleans at four in the afternoon, and it was "our watch" until eight. Mr. Bixby, my chief, "straightened her up," plowed her along past the sterns[12] of the other boats that lay at the Levee, and then said, "Here, take her; shave those steamships as close as you'd peel an apple." I took the wheel, and my heartbeat fluttered up into the hundreds; for it seemed to me that we were about to scrape the side off every ship in the line, we were so close. I held my breath and began to claw the boat away from the danger; and I had my own opinion of the pilot who had known no better than to get us into such peril, but I was too wise to express it. In half a minute I had a wide margin of safety intervening between the *Paul Jones* and the ships; and within ten seconds more I was set aside in disgrace, and Mr. Bixby was going into danger again and flaying me alive with abuse of my cowardice. I was stung, but I was obliged to admire the easy confidence with which my chief loafed from side to side of his wheel, and trimmed the ships so closely that disaster seemed ceaselessly imminent. When he had cooled a little he told me that the easy water was close ashore and the current outside, and therefore we must hug the bank, up-stream, to get the benefit of the former, and stay well out, down-

---

[12] *sterns*: rear ends of the boats

stream, to take advantage of the latter. In my own mind I resolved to be a down-stream pilot and leave the up-streaming to people dead to prudence.

Now and then Mr. Bixby called my attention to certain things. Said he, "This is Six-Mile Point." I assented. It was pleasant enough information, but I could not see the bearing of it. I was not conscious that it was a matter of any interest to me. Another time he said, "This is Nine-Mile Point." Later he said, "This is Twelve-Mile Point." They were all about level with the water's edge; they all looked about alike to me; they were monotonously unpicturesque. I hoped Mr. Bixby would change the subject. But no; he would crowd up around a point, hugging the shore with affection, and then say: "The slack water ends here, abreast this bunch of China trees; now we cross over." So he crossed over. He gave me the wheel once or twice, but I had no luck. I either came near chipping off the edge of a sugar-plantation, or I yawed too far from shore, and so dropped back into disgrace again and got abused.

The watch was ended at last, and we took supper and went to bed. At midnight the glare of a lantern shone in my eyes, and the night watchman said:

"Come, turn out!"

And then he left. I could not understand this extraordinary procedure; so I presently gave up trying to, and dozed off to sleep. Pretty soon the watchman was back again, and this time he was gruff. I was annoyed. I said:

"What do you want to come bothering around here in the middle of the night for? Now, as like as not, I'll not get to sleep again to-night."

The watchman said:

"Well, if this ain't good, I'm blessed."

The "off-watch" was just turning in, and I heard some brutal laughter from them, and such remarks as "Hello, watchman! ain't the new cub turned out yet? He's delicate, likely. Give him some sugar in a rag, and send for the chambermaid to sing 'Rock-a-by Baby,' to him."

About this time Mr. Bixby appeared on the scene. Something like a minute later I was climbing the pilot-house steps with some of my clothes on and the rest in my arms. Mr. Bixby was close behind, commenting. Here was something fresh—this thing of getting up in the middle of the night to go to work. It was a detail in piloting that had never occurred to me at all. I knew that boats ran all night, but somehow I had never happened to reflect that somebody had to get up out of a warm bed to run them. I began to fear that piloting was not quite so romantic as I had imagined it was; there was something very real and worklike about this new phase of it.

It was a rather dingy night, although a fair number of stars were out. The big mate was at the wheel, and he had the old tub pointed at a star and was holding her straight up the middle of the river. The shores on either hand were not much more than half a mile apart, but they seemed wonderfully far away and ever so vague and indistinct. The mate said:

"We've got to land at Jones's plantation, sir."

The vengeful spirit in me exulted. I said to myself, "I wish you joy of your job, Mr. Bixby; you'll have a good time finding Mr. Jones's plantation such a night as this; and I hope you never *will* find it as long as you live."

Mr. Bixby said to the mate:

"Upper end of the plantation, or the lower?"

"Upper."

"I can't do it. The stumps there are out of water at this stage. It's no great distance to the lower, and you'll have to get along with that."

"All right, sir. If Jones don't like it, he'll have to lump it, I reckon."

And then the mate left. My exultation began to cool and my wonder to come up. Here was a man who not only proposed to find this plantation on such a night, but to find either end of it you preferred. I dreadfully wanted to ask a question, but I was carrying about as many short answers as my cargo-room would admit of, so I held my peace. All I desired to ask Mr. Bixby was the simple question whether he was ass enough to really imagine he was going to find that plantation on a night when all plantations were exactly alike and all of the same color. But I held in. I used to have fine inspirations of prudence in those days.

Mr. Bixby made for the shore and soon was scraping it, just the same as if it had been daylight. And not only that, but singing:

"Father in heaven, the day is declining," etc.

It seemed to me that I had put my life in the keeping of a peculiarly reckless outcast. Presently he turned on me and said:

"What's the name of the first point above New Orleans?"

I was gratified to be able to answer promptly, and I did. I said I didn't know.

"Don't *know*?"

This manner jolted me. I was down at the foot again, in a moment. But I had to say just what I had said before.

"Well, you're a smart one!" said Mr. Bixby. "What's the name of the *next* point?"

Once more I didn't know.

"Well, this beats anything. Tell me the name of *any* point or place I told you."

I studied awhile and decided that I couldn't.

"Look here! What do you start out from, above Twelve-Mile Point, to cross over?"

"I—I—don't know."

"You—you—don't know?" mimicking my drawling manner of speech. "What *do* you know?"

"I—I—nothing, for certain."

"By the great Cæsar's[13] ghost, I believe you! You're the stupidest dunderhead I ever saw or ever heard of, so help me Moses! The idea of *you* being a pilot—*you!* Why, you don't know enough to pilot a cow down a lane."

Oh, but his wrath was up! He was a nervous man, and he shuffled from one side of his wheel to the other as if the floor was hot. He would boil awhile to himself, and then overflow and scald me again.

"Look here! What do you suppose I told you the names of those points for?"

I tremblingly considered a moment, and then the devil of temptation provoked me to say:

"Well to—to—be entertaining, I thought."

This was a red rag to the bull. He raged and stormed so (he was crossing the river at the time) that I judged it made him blind, because he ran over

---

[13] *Cæsar*: protagonist from William Shakespeare's play *Julius Cæsar*

the steering-oar of a trading-scow.[14] Of course the traders sent up a volley of red-hot profanity. Never was a man so grateful as Mr. Bixby was; because he was brimful, and here were subjects who could *talk back*. He threw open a window, thrust his head out, and such an irruption followed as I never had heard before. The fainter and farther away the scowmen's curses drifted, the higher Mr. Bixby lifted his voice and the weightier his adjectives grew. When he closed the window he was empty. You could have drawn a seine[15] through his system and not caught curses enough to disturb your mother with. Presently he said to me in the gentlest way:

"My boy, you must get a little memorandum-book; and every time I tell you a thing, put it down right away. There's only one way to be a pilot, and that is to get this entire river by heart. You have to know it just like A B C."

That was a dismal revelation to me; for my memory was never loaded with anything but blank cartridges. However, I did not feel discouraged long. I judged that it was best to make some allowances, for doubtless Mr. Bixby was "stretching." Presently he pulled a rope and struck a few strokes on the big

---

[14] *trading-scow*: a large, flat-bottomed boat used to transport materials such as coal and sand

[15] *seine*: a large net drawn in a circle by two boats to catch fish

bell. The stars were all gone now, and the night was as black as ink. I could hear the wheels churn along the bank, but I was not entirely certain that I could see the shore. The voice of the invisible watchman called up from the hurricane-deck:

"What's this, sir?"

"Jones's plantation."

I said to myself, "I wish I might venture to offer a small bet that it isn't." But I did not chirp. I only waited to see. Mr. Bixby handled the engine-bells, and in due time the boat's nose came to the land, a torch glowed from the forecastle, a man skipped ashore, a darky's voice on the bank said: "Gimme de k'yarpet-bag, Mass' Jones," and the next moment we were standing up the river again, all serene. I reflected deeply awhile, and then said—but not aloud—"Well, the finding of that plantation was the luckiest accident that ever happened; but it couldn't happen again in a hundred years." And I fully believed it *was* an accident, too.

By the time we had gone seven or eight hundred miles up the river, I had learned to be a tolerably plucky up-stream steersman, in daylight; and before we reached St. Louis I had made a trifle of progress in night work, but only a trifle. I had a note-book that fairly bristled with the names of towns, "points," bars, islands, bends, reaches, etc.; but the information was to be found only in the notebook—none of it was in my head. It made my heart ache to think I had only got half of the river set down; for as our watch was four hours off and four hours on, day and night, there was a long four-hour gap in my book for every time I had slept since the voyage began.

My chief was presently hired to go on a big New Orleans boat, and I packed my satchel and went with him. She was a grand affair. When I stood in her pilot-house I was so far above the water that I seemed perched on a mountain; and her decks stretched so far away, fore and aft, below me, that I wondered how I could ever have considered the little *Paul Jones* a large craft. There were other differences, too. The *Paul Jones's* pilot-house was a cheap, dingy, battered rattletrap, cramped for room; but here was a sumptuous glass temple; room enough to have a dance in; showy red and gold window-curtains; an imposing sofa; leather cushions and a back to the high bench where visiting pilots sit, to spin yarns and "look at the river"; bright, fanciful "cuspidores,"[16] instead of a broad wooden box filled with sawdust; nice new oilcloth on the floor; a hospitable big stove for winter; a wheel as high as my head, costly with inlaid work; a wire tiller-rope;

---

[16] *cuspidores*: spitoons

bright brass knobs for the bells; and a tidy, white-aproned, black "texas-tender," to bring up tarts and ices and coffee during mid-watch, day and night. Now this was "something like"; and so I began to take heart once more to believe that piloting was a romantic sort of occupation after all. The moment we were under way I began to prowl about the great steamer and fill myself with joy. She was as clean and as dainty as a drawing-room; when I looked down her long, gilded saloon, it was like gazing through a splendid tunnel; she had an oil-picture, by some gifted sign-painter, on every stateroom door; she glittered with no end of prism-fringed chandeliers; the clerk's office was elegant, the bar was marvelous, and the barkeeper had been barbered and upholstered at incredible cost. The boiler-deck (*i. e.*, the second story of the boat, so to speak) was as spacious as a church, it seemed to me; so with the forecastle; and there was no pitiful handful of deckhands, firemen, and roustabouts down there, but a whole battalion of men. The fires were fiercely glaring from a long row of furnaces, and over them were eight huge boilers! This was unutterable pomp. The mighty engines—but enough of this. I had never felt so fine before. And when I found that the regiment of natty servants respectfully "sir'd" me, my satisfaction was complete.

Mark Twain

Mark Twain, born Samuel Langhorne Clemens in 1835, grew up in Hannibal, Missouri. From the shores of that small river town, he viewed firsthand the traffic of the bustling steamboat industry, which moved goods and people up and down the great waterway. Like many of the other boys of Hannibal, Twain's dream was to work on a steamboat, but in the meantime, he spent his early years exploring local caves with his friends, playing pirates one day and bandits the next, and getting into typical boyhood mischief. But this carefree childhood ended at the age of 12 when his father died. To help support the family, Twain left school and became a printer's apprentice to his older brother, Orion, who had recently purchased a newspaper. He worked for Orion for six years but at the age of 18, decided to leave Hannibal.

Twain spent the next few years traveling from city to city working as a printer. When he was 21, he apprenticed himself to Horace Bixby, who taught him the art of steamboat piloting, and at 23, Twain received his pilot's license. Later, Twain would remember—and write about—those years with fondness, and it was, in fact, the leadsman's cry of "Mark twain!"—announcing a water depth of

12 feet—from which he gleaned his famous pen name.

In 1860, when the Civil War all but put an end to steamboating, Twain headed for the Nevada territory to try to make his fortune prospecting for gold. While he didn't discover much gold, he did find something else: a wealth of stories told by fellow prospectors around the campfires in mining camps. One such tale inspired him to write "The Celebrated Jumping Frog of Calaveras County," his first short story, published in 1865. Realizing he was better-suited to be a writer than a miner, Twain began working as journalist in Carson City, Nevada, and eventually took a job with a San Francisco newspaper.

In 1870, Twain married and moved to Hartford, Connecticut, where he continued his writing while raising three daughters. In 1876, Twain wrote *The Adventures of Tom Sawyer*, and in 1884, he produced *The Adventures of Huckleberry Finn*, generally considered to be a masterpiece in American fiction. The more Twain wrote, the more his fame seemed to grow, and eventually he became one of the most-often interviewed and photographed personalities of the 19th century.

Twain's life was not all fame and fortune, however. His later years were marked by financial losses, professional disappointment, and personal tragedy. At one point, he lost more than $200,000 when he invested in an impractical typesetting machine. In order to pay his debt, he was forced to embark on long, arduous nationwide lecture tours, which taxed his health and robbed him of time to write. While he produced *A Connecticut Yankee in King Arthur's Court* in 1889 and *Pudd'nhead Wilson* in 1894, neither was as successful as *Huckleberry Finn*. But the most devastating events occurred between 1902 and 1909 with the death of his wife and two of his daughters. By that time, Twain himself had developed heart disease, causing his energy to decline as he struggled to complete new works. In 1910, just four months after losing his second daughter, Twain died. He left behind one daughter and a literary legacy that lives on today. His works have been translated into 72 languages, and Mark Twain associations exist all over the world, devoted to keeping his writings alive.

FROM *LIFE ON THE MISSISSIPPI*

I. THE STORY LINE
A. Digging for Facts

1. When Mark Twain leaves Cincinnati, his intentions are to (a) prospect for gold, (b) explore the mouth of the Amazon, (c) become a steamboat pilot.

2. While traveling on the *Paul Jones*, Twain actually imitates the "cub"-engineer he saw as a young boy in Hannibal by (a) purposely showing off in front of country boys on the banks, (b) swearing and acting as if he owns the boat, (c) dressing in fancy clothing.

3. The stories the night watchman tells young Twain (a) impress Twain but turn out to be false, (b) cause Twain to want to be a night watchman, (c) cause Twain to hesitate about working on a steamboat

4. Before meeting Horace Bixby, Twain believed that steamboat piloting consisted mostly of (a) keeping one's boat in the middle of the river, (b) taking it easy in the boat's pilot house, (c) being admired by the crew and passengers, especially the ladies.

5. The first thing young Twain does when given the boat's wheel is to (a) run the *Paul Jones* into another boat, (b) run over the front end of a trading scow, (c) put a wide margin between the *Paul Jones* and the other ships.

6. One of first things that makes Twain realize that piloting isn't all that romantic is that he must (a) carry out the lowly duties of a cabin boy, (b) wake up in the middle of the night to serve watch, (c) eat his food with the rest of the crew.

7. When Bixby questions Twain about the various points of the river, Twain replies with (a) "I don't know," (b) the correct answer every time, (c) guesses.

8. Twain believes that Bixby's ability to find the Jones's plantation in the darkness is (a) pure luck, (b) something he'll be able to do one day, (c) an easy task if one knows the river.

9. Bixby advises Twain to (a) find another occupation, (b) write things down in a notebook, (c) go back to Hannibal.

10. When Bixby is transferred to another boat, Twain (a) goes with him, (b) continues his training with the new pilot on the *Paul Jones*, (c) seeks out another pilot to train him.

B. Probing for Theme

A *theme* is a central message of a piece of literature. Read the thematic statements below. Which one best applies to these excerpts from Mark Twain's *Life on the Mississippi*? Be prepared to support your opinion.

1. Romantic notions are often blind to reality.
2. If one works hard enough, one can obtain any goal.
3. Naïve people are often taken advantage of.

II. IN SEARCH OF MEANING

1. How does the village of Hannibal change when the steamboats arrive? What is it like before and after the arrivals?
2. Explain the attitude Mark Twain and the other boys of Hannibal have toward members of steamboat crews.
3. What does Twain admire about the "big stormy mate"? Why do you think the mate reacts as he does to Twain's offer of help?

4. How does the night watchman come up with the fantastic tales he tells Twain? How might Twain know that the tales are false?

5. What kind of person is the young man who borrows money from Twain? How might Twain have figured this out before lending him the money?

6. Why doesn't Twain pursue his dream of exploring the mouth of the Amazon? Do you think the dream is a practical one? Explain.

7. What does Mr. Bixby do that causes Twain to doubt Bixby's capabilities? How do Bixby's actions prove that he is a very capable pilot?

8. Why do you think Mr. Bixby doesn't tell Twain he has to wake up in the middle of the night for his watch?

9. Why does Mr. Bixby advise Twain to keep a notebook? Why is Twain dissatisfied with the amount of information it contains by the time the boat had traveled 700 or 800 miles up the river?

10. Why does Twain attribute Bixby's finding the Jones's plantation to luck? What does this tell you about Twain at this point?

III. DEVELOPING WORD POWER

Exercise A

Each of the following words appears in a sentence taken directly from the selection in this book. Read the sentence, and then select the correct meaning from the four choices.

1. transient

   "We had *transient* ambitions of other sorts, but they were only transient."

   a. impractical   c. youthful
   b. admirable   d. temporary

2. prodigious

   "Presently a film of dark smoke appears above one of those remote 'points': instantly a negro drayman, famous for his quick eye and *prodigious* voice, lifts up the cry . . . "

   a. melodious   c. deep
   b. tremendous   d. harsh

3. obscurity

"That boy had been notoriously worldly, and I just the reverse; yet he was exalted to this [position of respect], and I left in *obscurity* and misery."

a. sadness
b. oblivion
c. disgrace
d. envy

4. ignoble

"I was in such a glorified condition that all *ignoble* feelings departed out of me, and I was able to look down and pity the untraveled with a compassion that had hardly a trace of contempt in it."

a. angry
b. dishonorable
c. doubtful
d. unforgiving

5. abstruse

"Then he said impressively: 'Well, if this don't beat h—l!' and turned to his work with the air of a man who had been confronted with a problem too *abstruse* for solution."

a. complex
b. ridiculous
c. horrible
d. unworthy

6. sublime

"He was huge and muscular, his face was bearded and whiskered all over; he had a red woman and a blue woman tattooed on his right arm—one on each side of a blue anchor with a red rope to it; and in the matter of profanity he was *sublime*."

a. shocking
b. educated
c. entertaining
d. inspiring

7. homage

"He could not well have helped it, I hung with such *homage* on his words and so plainly showed that I felt honored by his notice."

a. respect
b. attentiveness
c. persistence
d. tenderness

8. plaintive

"As he mellowed into his *plaintive* history his tears dripped upon the lantern in his lap, and I cried, too, from sympathy."

a. drawn-out
b. false
c. ancient
d. mournful

9. imminent

"I was stung, but I was obliged to admire the easy confidence with which my chief loafed from side to side of his wheel, and trimmed the ships so closely that disaster seem ceaselessly *imminent.*"

a. avoidable
b. terrifying
c. approaching
d. necessary

10. prudence

"In my own mind I resolved to be a down-stream pilot and leave the up-streaming to people dead to *prudence.*"

a. advice
b. reality
c. good judgment
d. fear

Exercise B

Below is a list of vocabulary words (or a form of each) from the selection. Choose the word that best completes the sentences that follow the list.

- a. abstruse
- b. homage
- c. ignoble
- d. imminent
- e. obscurity
- f. plaintive
- g. prodigious
- h. prudence
- i. transient
- j. sublime

1. Knowing that winter was __?__ , Mrs. Schmidt filled her cellar with canned fruits and vegetables.

2. "Since life is __?__ , we should make the most of each day," the philosopher said.

3. The principal's __?__ voice frightened some of the younger students.

4. "You acted with __?__ when you decided to leave the unsupervised party," Mr. Malik told his daughter.

5. The presence of the bishop seemed to create a __?__ atmosphere at the memorial service.

6. "The __?__ voice of the nightingale always makes me sad," Denise told her friend.

7. After his first hit single, the rock singer seemed to vanish into __?__.

8. Every year millions of people visit the Vietnam memorial to pay __?__ to the 58,000 men and women who lost their lives.

9. "In order to be a charitable person, one must banish all __?__ thoughts about others," the pastor said.

10. The crime was so __?__ that police were sure a seasoned criminal had planned it.

FROM *LIFE ON THE MISSISSIPPI*

IV. IMPROVING WRITING SKILLS

Exercise A

Choose one of the following activities.

1. In these excerpts, Mark Twain is a *naïve*, or unknowing, narrator. In other words, the reader knows more about some of the events Twain describes than Twain does. For example, Twain thinks the young man he encountered when he boarded the *Paul Jones* doesn't pay back the six dollars Twain lent him because he forgot or died. The reader knows that the young man purposely cheated Twain out of the money. Write a paper in which you discuss other instances where Twain is a naïve narrator. In each case, explain what the reader knows and what Twain does not know. Then explain whether you think the use of a naïve narrator adds or detracts from the story.

2. Write a character sketch of Mr. Bixby. Include a description of his character as well as a physical description as you see him in your mind. (Keep in mind that he was only 32 years old when he trained Twain.)

Exercise B

1. Create the notebook Mr. Bixby advises Twain to keep. Based on the selection and your own imagination, make entries in the notebook as Twain might have. Include any personal comment you think he might have included.

2. Write an advertisement Mr. Bixby may have written for a cub-pilot. Include the qualities he might have looked for in a candidate and the experience he may have required.

V. THINGS TO WRITE OR TALK ABOUT

1. Why do you think steamboat piloting was so admired by young boys in Twain's time? What occupations might be considered "romantic," or idealistic, today? What might be some of the realities of those occupations?

2. How does Twain use humor to relate his tale?

3. Mr. Bixby often "flays" Twain alive during his training. Do you think Mr. Bixby expects too much of Twain? Why do you think Twain sticks with his training? What qualities does he possess that help him succeed in becoming a pilot?

FROM *LIFE ON THE MISSISSIPPI*

4. A *romantic* is a person who has an idealistic outlook; he or she sees things as better than they are. In what ways is young Mark Twain a romantic? Explain whether you think his romantic views help him or harm him in becoming a steamboat pilot.

5. Twain wrote this story as an older adult looking back on his younger years. What advantages are there to looking back at an event that happened many years before? What disadvantages might there be?

ANSWER KEY

I. THE STORY LINE
A. Digging for Facts

1. b
2. a
3. a
4. a
5. c
6. b
7. a
8. a
9. b
10. a

B. Probing for Theme

Students may elect to support any of the three choices. The suggested answer is *Romantic notions are often blind to reality.* Twain believes that the crew members of the boats that docked at Hannibal have only enjoyable duties when in reality they probably perform many unpleasant tasks. He also believes that he can go to South America with very little forethought; he soon learns that few ships ever made that voyage, possibly because it is long, dangerous, and impractical. Twain thinks a pilot's job is easy; he is amazed to find out that he is expected to know the river's current and all of its points and landmarks, and that he has to wake up in the middle of the night to work.

III. DEVELOPING WORD POWER
Exercise A

1. transient
   d. temporary

2. prodigious
   b. tremendous

3. obscurity
   b. oblivion

4. ignoble
   b. dishonorable

5. abstruse
   a. complex

6. sublime
   d. inspiring

7. homage
   a. respect

8. plaintive

    d. mournful

9. imminent

    c. approaching

10. prudence

    c. good judgment

Exercise B

1. (d)   imminent
2. (i)   transient
3. (g)   prodigious
4. (h)   prudence
5. (j)   sublime
6. (f)   plaintive
7. (e)   obscurity
8. (b)   homage
9. (c)   ignoble
10. (a) abstruse